Encouraging Words for Mothers

E5085

305800232125

Warner Press, Inc.

Warner Press and Warner Press logo are trademarks of Warner Press, Inc.

Editors: Robin Loisch, Julie Campbell
Cover and Layout by Katie Miller

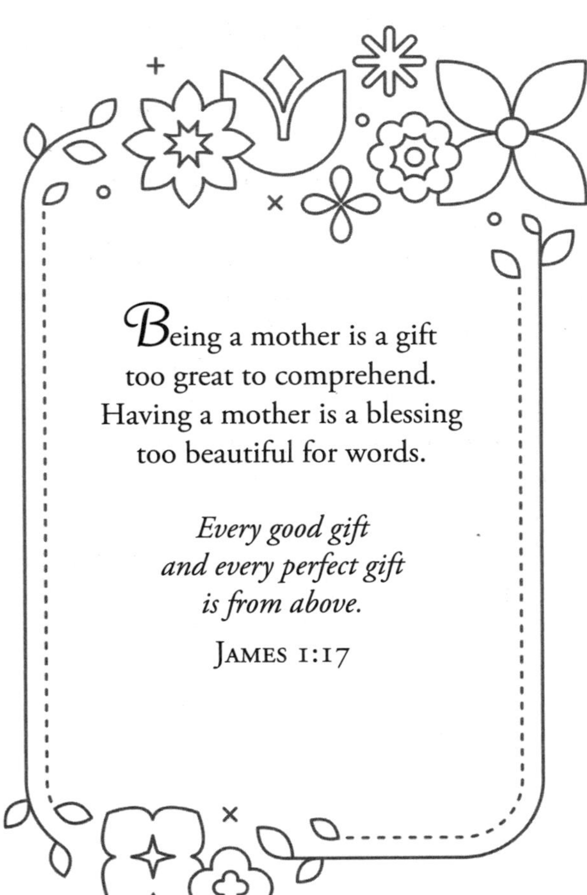

Being a mother is a gift
too great to comprehend.
Having a mother is a blessing
too beautiful for words.

Every good gift
and every perfect gift
is from above.

JAMES 1:17

Maternal Love

Many of us are blessed to have moms who applied bandages to our scraped knees when we were young, or spoke the exact words we needed to hear when we were struggling. Others of us, by the grace of God, came to experience maternal figures in our lives, from the aunt who made us laugh, to the mom-mentor at church who hugged us and called us her "kids." For all of us, we have an eternal God who cares for us in maternal ways. When we're hurting, God reminds us, *As a mother comforts her child, so will I comfort you* (Isaiah 66:13 NIV). God longs to gather us to Him *as a hen gathers her chicks under her wings* (Luke 13:34 NIV). God delights in His children and rejoices over them with singing (see Zephaniah 3:17). Today let's be thankful for maternal love, whether in human or divine form.

Tammy Tilley

Motherhood is
a partnership
with God.

Author Unknown

Unless the Lord builds the house,
its builders labor in vain.

Psalm 127:1 (NIV)

A Mother's Creed

I will worry less about my children
and trust God more.

I will commit them into the Lord's care.

I will love my children unconditionally and
let them know I do.

I will believe in them constantly
and encourage them often.

I will pray for them daily.

I will teach them responsibility
for their own actions.

I will try to be an example of godliness,
but I will be unafraid to let them see my faults.

I will give them generous doses of laughter,
interspersed with fun.

I will release them when they are grown,
but they will always be my own.

Rebecca Barlow Jordan

Home is wherever
your mother is.

Where your treasure is,
there will your heart be also.

Matthew 6:21

A Mother's Faith

When I was eight years old, my mom was diagnosed with a rare form of cancer. My little mind was constantly racing, wondering what would happen to my beloved mommy. As a woman of great faith, my mom trusted God's will for her life, no matter the outcome. Thankfully, God eventually chose to heal her of cancer. Seeing my mom's faith during this trial and wondering about my own standing with God led me to accept Christ at a young age. Mothers, never underestimate your influence over your children, especially in the face of problems and trials. They are watching, and by your example, you have the privilege of pointing them to Jesus.

Julie Campbell

The deepest fountains of love

*are found at the cross of Christ
and in a mother's heart.*

Author Unknown

*My dear children,
let's not just talk about love;
let's practice real love. This is the only way
we'll know we're living truly,
living in God's reality.*

1 JOHN 3:18 (MSG)

On the day we are born,
God gives each of us
a beautiful guardian angel;
and as we grow,
we give her a name…
Mother.

For he shall give his angels
charge over thee,
to keep thee in all thy ways.

Psalm 91:11

A mother's love
reaches far beyond
circumstances and feelings....

It sees past flaws and imperfections…
and celebrates God's gift of love,
sent from heaven in the form of a child.

Children are a gift from the L*ORD;*
they are a reward from him.

PSALM 127:3 (NLT)

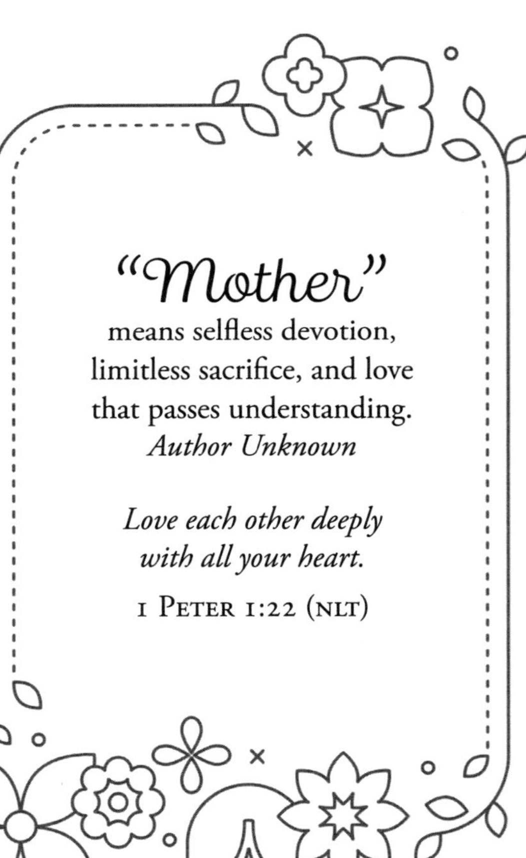

“Mother”

means selfless devotion,
limitless sacrifice, and love
that passes understanding.

Author Unknown

Love each other deeply
with all your heart.

1 Peter 1:22 (NLT)

My Mother's Hands

They were endlessly willing
to tie loose shoelaces,
make building block towers,
and wipe tears from small faces.
And they never grew tired
of mending old teddy bears,
clapping for recitals,
or winding ribbons through hair.
Yet in their lifetime of service,
the sweetest blessing I find
is her precious hands folded
in prayer next to mine.

Kimberly K. Smith

For the mother is and must be,
whether she knows it or not,
the greatest, strongest,
and most lasting teacher
her children have.

Hannah Whitall Smith

Train up a child
in the way he should go:
and when he is old,
he will not depart from it.

PROVERBS 22:6

Following the Leader

One morning I was leading preschool Sunday school children in the song "Deep and Wide." In the middle of making hand motions for "wide," my nose was itching, so I reached up to scratch it. All of the children did the same thing! What a powerful lesson. At that moment I realized how much influence I had on the little ones entrusted to me. They were looking up to me; I was setting an example for them to follow. Just as Jesus said, *Suffer the little children to come unto me* (Mark 10:14), we also are responsible for teaching children by our everyday actions. They are watching us as examples of Christ. This simple but powerful little lesson has stayed with me through raising my children and now my grandchildren. Sometimes the best lessons in life are the simplest.

Kathryn Stoops

No ordinary work done
by a man is either as hard
or as responsible
as the work of a mother who is
bringing up a family
of small children...
for upon her time and strength
demands are made not only
every hour of the day but often
every hour of the night.

President Theodore Roosevelt

No gift to your mother can ever equal her gift to you—life.

Oh yes, you shaped me first inside, then out;
you formed me in my mother's womb....
You know every bone in my body;
You know exactly how I was made, bit by bit,
how I was sculpted from nothing into something.
Like an open book, you watched me grow
from conception to birth; all the stages of my life
were spread out before you, The days of my life
all prepared before I'd even lived one day.

Psalm 139:13-16 (MSG)

Celebrate Motherhood

Every mom visualizes the moment when her perfect baby will be born—the joy of her heart and life. But the first sounds she hears are not the sweet cooing of a contented infant, but the sharp wails of a screaming stranger. Years that follow may bring a love-hate tug of war between "I love you always," and a "Who is this child anyway?" Yet in spite of child-rearing difficulties, most women would agree: No joy compares to that of being a mother. No matter how deep the pain, no matter her losses or gain, these children are still flesh of her flesh. God pushes the pain into the background and ushers joy to the forefront of a mother's heart. Just like God's unconditional love that says, *I have loved thee with an everlasting love* (Jeremiah 31:3), a mother can never sever her love for her child.

Rebecca Barlow Jordan

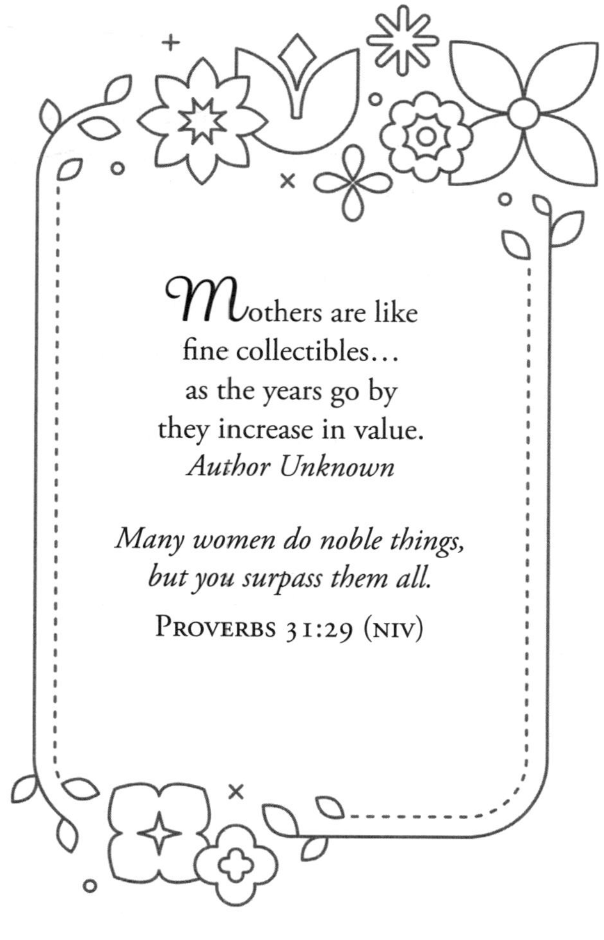

Mothers are like
fine collectibles…
as the years go by
they increase in value.
Author Unknown

*Many women do noble things,
but you surpass them all.*

Proverbs 31:29 (NIV)

Even He that died for us upon the cross,
in the last hour, in the unutterable agony of death,
was mindful of His mother, as if to teach us
that this holy love should be our
last worldly thought—
the last point of earth
from which the soul should take
its flight for heaven.

Henry Wadsworth Longfellow

*When Jesus saw his mother there,
and the disciple whom he loved standing nearby,
he said to her, "Woman, here is your son,"
and to the disciple, "Here is your mother."
From that time on,
this disciple took her into his home.*

John 19:26–27 (niv)

A Debt of Love

When we think of debt, we usually think of money, but the Bible states, *Let no debt remain outstanding, except the continuing debt to love one another* (Romans 13:8, NIV). Who deserves an "installment" of that love more than mothers? Mothers aren't usually recognized for promotions or new positions, they don't receive a salary, but they are the single most powerful work force on the planet. In the homes where they serve every day, personalities are molded, future parents are trained, and the leaders of the next generation are formed. Mothers serve tirelessly and selflessly—so let's reward them with love.

A Mother's Harvest

Mothers are a lot like farmers. They nurture seedling children into adulthood, watering, tilling, caring for the young "plants" with tender attention. Yet many mothers wonder if they will ever see a "harvest" as they face day after day of diapers, dust, and dishwater. Galatians assures mothers that *we will reap a harvest if we do not give up* (6:9, NIV). The true reward of a mother's toil is the sum of a child's life and her involvement there. All the hurts, the joys, the pain, and the happiness somehow add up to something wonderful with the help of God and a mother who cares. May He give you the ability to rejoice in the daily blessings and burdens that contribute to the ongoing harvest of your child's life!

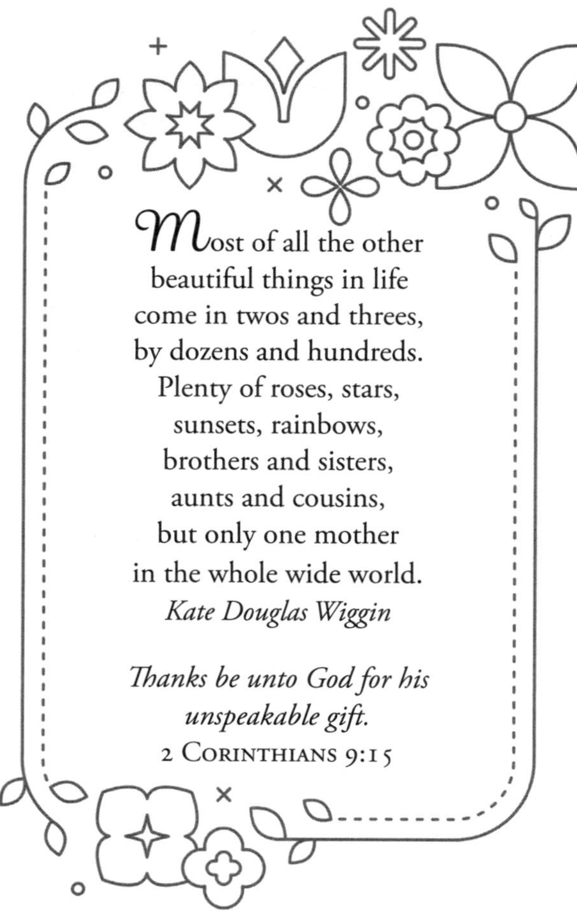

Most of all the other
beautiful things in life
come in twos and threes,
by dozens and hundreds.
Plenty of roses, stars,
sunsets, rainbows,
brothers and sisters,
aunts and cousins,
but only one mother
in the whole wide world.
Kate Douglas Wiggin

*Thanks be unto God for his
unspeakable gift.*
2 Corinthians 9:15

A Binding Love

A mother's love is a continuing gift. Young children look to their mothers for care and protection as they grow. Moms also become role models and confidantes. And when kids become adults, mothers can be best friends and sources of strength during difficult times. During our life, we will encounter rocky times, but having someone by our side can make the journey easier. As Christians we know that Jesus walks beside us and that His love binds us to Him and to each other. In Ecclesiastes 4:12 we read, *A cord of three strands is not quickly broken* (NIV). As we share life's journey with our mothers, God is the third strand that binds us together. As we celebrate the gift of a mother's love, let us also remember the One whose ultimate gift makes it all possible.

Motherhood is a work of heart.

I prayed for this child, and the Lord
has granted me what I asked of him.
So now I give him to the Lord.
For his whole life he will be given
over to the Lord.

1 Samuel 1:27-28 (niv)

A Virtuous Woman

Is there a mom among us who really feels like she measures up to the Proverbs 31 woman? It's not hard to look at this woman who sews, runs a business, cooks, farms, sells, etc. and say, "How can I ever measure up to her?" Thank goodness God's Spirit is here to help us! As Scripture assures us, *My grace is sufficient for thee* (2 Corinthians 12:9). With God's help, we can be the best moms we can be. Though we may not do all the things the supermom in Proverbs did, if we lean on the Lord, He will make us the strong, solid, loving, and faithful mothers that our children need so much.

No language can express the power and beauty and heroism and majesty of a mother's love. It shrinks not where man cowers, and grows stronger where man faints.

E. H. Chapin

Let us, your servants, see you work again; let our children see your glory. And may the Lord our God show us his approval and make our efforts successful. Yes, make our efforts successful!

PSALM 90:16-17 (NLT)

A mother is the truest friend we have, when trials heavy and sudden, fall upon us; when adversity takes the place of prosperity; when friends who rejoice with us in our sunshine desert us; when trouble thickens around us, still will she cling to us, and endeavor by her kind precepts and counsels to dissipate the clouds of darkness, and cause peace to return to our hearts.

Washington Irving

Love's Silhouette

Those who have known the joy of having a Christian mother are truly blessed. Her love is a glorious reflection of the love God has for us. A mother's love always holds us close, nurturing us and softening the harsh realities of life. From our toddler years, through rebellious teenage years, and on through adulthood, a godly mother's love for us never fades. In fact, any mother will tell you that even when her child is in his forties, she still sees him as that precious baby boy she rocked in the cradle—her love for her child is still as tender as it was all those years ago. A mother's love for her children is priceless, but even more so is her love for God. How many times has the sight of a mother praying and reading her Bible touched the heart of a wayward child, leading the child home once again. Though she may not fully realize it, a mother's faithfulness to God leaves a lasting impression on her children.

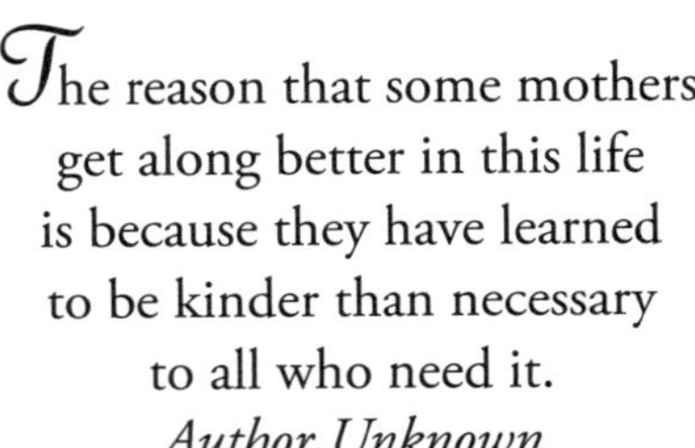

The reason that some mothers
get along better in this life
is because they have learned
to be kinder than necessary
to all who need it.
Author Unknown

*Be kind and compassionate
to one another,
forgiving each other,
just as in Christ
God forgave you.*

Ephesians 4:32 (NIV)

A Good Mother

Anybody can be a mom who is biologically qualified, but there is much more to mothering than delivering a baby and caring for its physical needs. Even the youngest child needs a mother who gives of herself emotionally and commits herself to prayer for her child's future. A mother must be able to discern between defiance and childlike irresponsibility, so that her child receives proper discipline. She must guard a child's tender heart with all that is in her, and make clear what sin is with the same conviction. She must model our heavenly Father's heart not only through Biblical teaching, but with a holy lifestyle of her own. The famous passage in Proverbs 31 tells what the reward of a good mother is: *Her children arise up, and call her blessed* (verse 28).

A mother's love gives us
our first glimpse of heaven.

You brought me safely
from my mother's womb
and led me to trust you
at my mother's breast.
I was thrust into your arms
at my birth.
You have been my God
from the moment I was born.

Psalm 22:9-10 (NLT)

Homemade Gifts

A mother cherishes her young child's handmade cards. She does not care if the shapes are indistinguishable and the spelling a bit "creative." Homemade gifts are often the best because of the love that went into making them. God also wants a homemade gift—our hearts. Nothing we could buy, no monetary investment in God's kingdom, would please God more than simply giving ourselves. Christ said the greatest commandment is to *love the Lord thy God with all thy heart, and with all thy soul, and with all thy mind, and with all thy strength* (Mark 12:30). Tell God of your love today.

I remember my mother's prayers

and they have always followed me.
They have clung to me all my life.

Abraham Lincoln

Do not be anxious about anything,
but in every situation,
by prayer and petition, with thanksgiving,
present your requests to God.
And the peace of God,
which transcends all understanding,
will guard your hearts and your minds
in Christ Jesus.

PHILIPPIANS 4:6-7 (NIV)

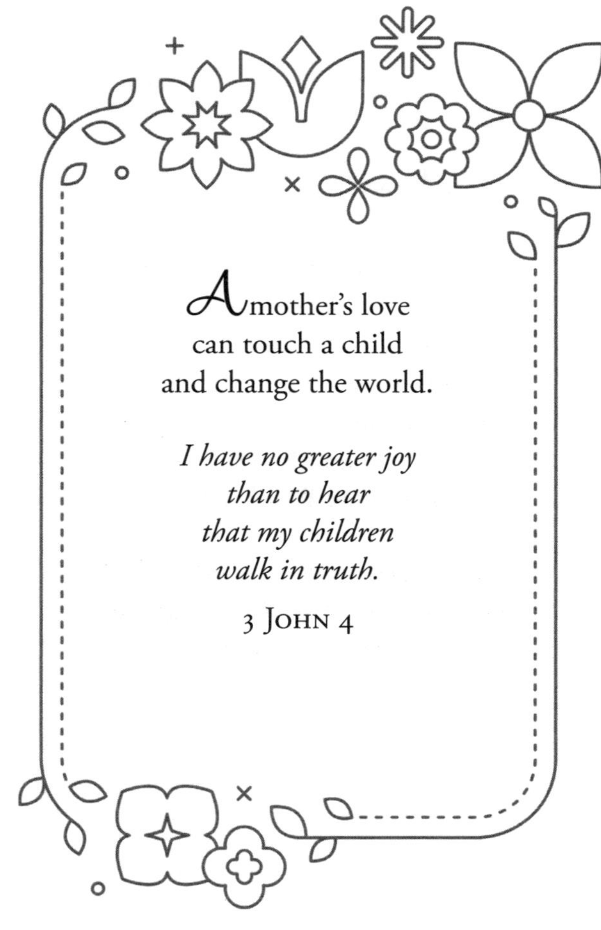

A mother's love
can touch a child
and change the world.

*I have no greater joy
than to hear
that my children
walk in truth.*

3 John 4

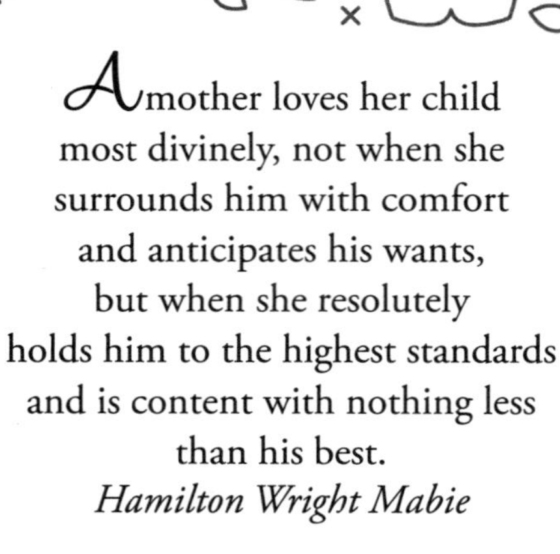

A mother loves her child
most divinely, not when she
surrounds him with comfort
and anticipates his wants,
but when she resolutely
holds him to the highest standards
and is content with nothing less
than his best.
Hamilton Wright Mabie

Whatsoever ye do in word or deed,
do all in the name of the Lord Jesus.
COLOSSIANS 3:17

A mother holds her children's hands for a while, but their hearts forever.

Author Unknown

Her children arise and call her blessed;
her husband also, and he praises her.
Proverbs 31:28 (NIV)

A mother is someone who
dreams great dreams for you,
but then she lets you chase
the dreams you have for yourself
and loves you just the same.

Author Unknown

*We know that all things work
together for good to them
that love God, to them who are
the called according to his purpose.*
Romans 8:28

If children have their mother's love, they have all they really need.

Many waters cannot quench love,
neither can the floods drown it.

Song of Solomon 8:7

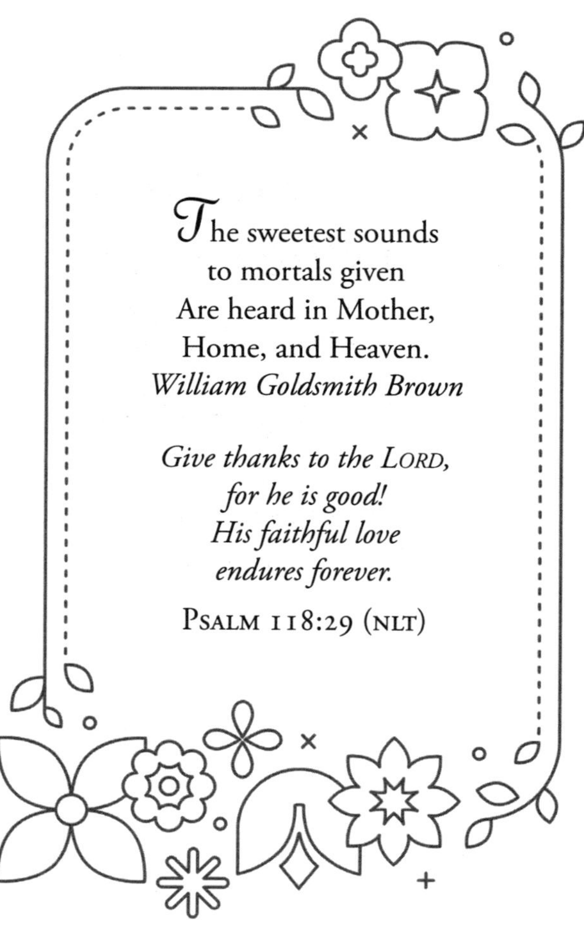

The sweetest sounds
to mortals given
Are heard in Mother,
Home, and Heaven.
William Goldsmith Brown

Give thanks to the LORD,
for he is good!
His faithful love
endures forever.

PSALM 118:29 (NLT)

A mother's love endures through all;

in good repute, in bad repute, in the face
of the world's condemnation
a mother still loves on.
Washington Irving

Love is patient, love is kind.
It does not envy, it does not boast, it is not proud.
It does not dishonor others, it is not self-seeking,
it is not easily angered, it keeps no record of wrongs.
Love does not delight in evil but rejoices with the truth.
It always protects, always trusts, always hopes,
always perseveres. Love never fails.

1 Corinthians 13:4-8 (NIV)

Mothers make memories the heart keeps forever.

Read up on what happened before you were born; dig into the past, understand your roots. Ask your parents what it was like before you were born.

Deuteronomy 32:7 (msg)

Nobody knows of the work it makes
To keep the home together.
Nobody knows of the steps it takes;
Nobody knows but Mother.
Anonymous

*Reward her for all she has done.
Let her deeds publicly declare
her praise.*
PROVERBS 31:31 (NLT)

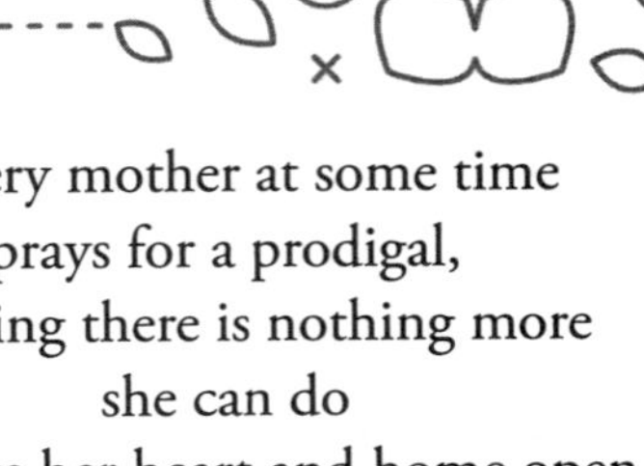

Every mother at some time
prays for a prodigal,
knowing there is nothing more
she can do
but leave her heart and home open
to the hope of the Lord.

Author Unknown

Choose you this day whom
ye will serve...
but as for me and my house,
we will serve the Lord.

Joshua 24:15

God gives us the gift of life, wrapped in a mother's love.

Before I shaped you in the womb,
I knew all about you.
Before you saw the light of day,
I had holy plans for you.

Jeremiah 1:5 (MSG)

Mothers Forever

No matter your age or the stage in your children's development, once you are a mother, you're a mother forever. God places within each mom the need to nurture her little ones, always guiding, always loving, always giving and prodding them in the right direction with gentle reminders: "Be careful," "Dress warmly," "Eat healthy." The years pass, and instead of motherhood ending, it begins a new role, another title: Grandmother. Same loving, same nurturing, same prodding in the right direction—only with a bit more spoiling! At some point it may appear you've changed roles completely, as your now grown child mothers you. Not so. Because inside, where it really counts, a mom never changes: she's always guiding, always loving, always giving.

Rebecca Barlow Jordan

All that I am, or hope to be,
I owe to my angel mother.

Abraham Lincoln

May our Lord Jesus Christ himself
and God our Father, who loved us
and by his grace gave us eternal
encouragement and good hope,
encourage your hearts
and strengthen you
in every good deed and word.

2 Thessalonians 2:16-17 (niv)

Loving mothers mirror Christ's compassion.

Charm is deceptive, and beauty is fleeting;
but a woman who fears the LORD *is to be praised.*

PROVERBS 31:30 (NIV)